● Start TO Finish
Second Series

FROM Wax TO Crayon

● ROBIN NELSON

LERNER PUBLICATIONS ⟩ Minneapolis

Lerner Publications Company
A division of Lerner Publishing Group, Inc.
241 First Avenue North
Minneapolis, MN 55401 USA

For reading levels and more information, look up this title at www.lernerbooks.com.

Photo Acknowledgments
The images in this book are used with the permission of: AP Photo/Steve Klaver, pp. 1, 9, 11; © Svitlana Kataieva/ Shutterstock.com, p. 3; © Philip Scalia/Alamy, p. 5; © William Thomas Cain/Stringer/Getty Images, pp. 7, 17, 19; A36609 Daniel Karmann Deutsch Presse Agentur/ Newscom, p. 13; AP Photo/Rick Smith, p. 15; © Robert Pernell/Shutterstock.com, p. 21; © Digital Vision/Getty Images, p. 23.

Front cover: © Peter Morley/Shutterstock.com.

Main body text set in Arta Std Book 20/26.
Typeface provided by International Typeface Corp.

Library of Congress Cataloging-in-Publication Data

Nelson, Robin, 1971–
    From wax to crayon / by Robin Nelson.
        p.   cm. — (Start to finish, second series. Everyday products)
    Audience: Grades K to 3.
    Includes index.
    ISBN 978–0–7613–9183–8 (lib. bdg. : alk. paper)
    ISBN 978–1–4677–1042–8 (EB pdf)
    1. Crayons—Juvenile literature. 2. Wax-modeling—Juvenile literature. I. Title.
TS1268.N45 2013
665'.4—dc23   2012007923

Manufactured in the United States of America
7-44803-12710-10/5/2017

TABLE OF Contents

I color with crayons. How are they made?

Wax melts.

Crayons start as clear wax. Wax is made into crayons at a **factory**. Large tanks heat the wax. The wax melts into a gooey liquid.

A worker adds color.

Pipes carry the clear wax into many pots called **vats**. A worker adds colored powder called **pigment** to the vats. A different color is stirred into each vat.

The wax is shaped.

The colored wax is poured into a **mold**. The mold has many holes. Each hole is shaped like a crayon. The wax fills the holes.

The wax gets hard.

Cold water flows under the mold. It cools the wax. Cooling makes the wax hard. The wax becomes crayons.

A worker checks the crayons.

The crayons are taken out of the mold. A worker checks each crayon for chips or dents. Crayons with chips or dents will be melted and molded again.

A machine wraps the crayons.

The crayons are sent into a machine that spins. It wraps each crayon in a piece of paper. The paper is called a **label**. The label tells the name of the crayon's color.

A machine sorts the crayons.

Crayons of the same color line up in the slots of a sorting machine. The machine sorts the crayons into sets. A set has crayons of different colors.

The crayons are boxed.

A packing machine puts the sets into boxes. Some boxes have just a few crayons. Some boxes have crayons of every color the factory makes.

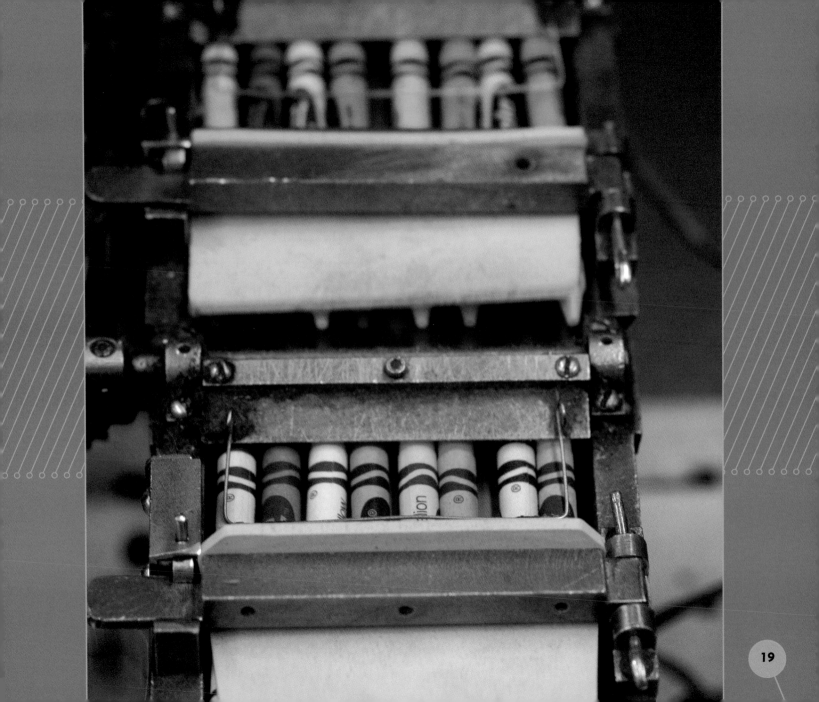

The crayons are sent to stores.

A worker fills large cartons with boxes of crayons. The cartons are packed onto a truck. The truck takes the crayons to stores.

I draw pictures with many colors!

People buy crayons at the store. My crayon box has many colors. What should I draw?

Glossary

factory (FAK-tuh-ree): a building where things are made

label (LAY-buhl): a paper that names a crayon's color

mold (MOHLD): a container that shapes crayons

pigment (PIHG-mehnt): a powder that colors wax

vats (VATS): pots for melting wax

Index